Stage-Land

Jerome K. Jerome

Contents

THE HERO.	7
THE VILLAIN.	12
THE HEROINE.	17
THE COMIC MAN.	21
THE LAWYER.	26
THE ADVENTURESS.	30
THE SERVANT-GIRL.	35
THE CHILD.	39
THE COMIC LOVERS.	44
THE PEASANTS.	48
THE GOOD OLD MAN.	52
THE IRISHMAN.	54
THE DETECTIVE.	57
THE SAILOR.	59

STAGE-LAND

BY

Jerome K. Jerome

THE HERO.

His name is George, generally speaking. "Call me George!" he says to the heroine. She calls him George (in a very low voice, because she is so young and timid). Then he is happy.

The stage hero never has any work to do. He is always hanging about and getting into trouble. His chief aim in life is to be accused of crimes he has never committed, and if he can muddle things up with a corpse in some complicated way so as to get himself reasonably mistaken for the murderer, he feels his day has not been wasted.

He has a wonderful gift of speech and a flow of language calculated to strike terror to the bravest heart. It is a grand thing to hear him bullyragging the villain.

The stage hero is always entitled to "estates," chiefly remarkable for their high state of cultivation and for the eccentric ground plan of the "manor house" upon them. The house is never more than one story high, but it makes up in green stuff over the porch what it lacks in size and convenience.

The chief drawback in connection with it, to our eyes, is that all the inhabitants of the neighboring village appear to live in the front garden, but the hero evidently thinks it rather nice of them, as it enables him to make speeches to them from the front doorstep--his favorite recreation.

There is generally a public-house immediately opposite. This is handy.

These "estates" are a great anxiety to the stage hero. He is not what you would call a business man, as far as we can judge, and his attempts to manage his own property invariably land him in ruin and distraction. His "estates," however, always get taken away from him by the villain before the first act is over, and this saves him all further trouble with regard to them until the end of the play, when he gets saddled with them once more.

Not but what it must be confessed that there is much excuse for the poor fellow's general bewilderment concerning his affairs and for his legal errors and confusions generally. Stage "law" may not be quite the most fearful and wonderful mystery in the whole universe, but it's near it--very near it. We were under the impression at one time that we ourselves knew something--just a little--about statutory and common law, but after paying attention to the legal points of one or two plays we found that we were mere children at it.

We thought we would not be beaten, and we determined to get to the bottom of stage law and to understand it; but after some six months' effort our brain (a singularly fine one) began to soften, and we abandoned the study, believing it would come cheaper in the end to offer a suitable reward, of about 50,000 pounds or 60,000 pounds, say, to any one who would explain it to us.

The reward has remained unclaimed to the present day and is still open.

One gentleman did come to our assistance a little while ago, but his explanations only made the matter more confusing to our minds than it was before. He was surprised at what he called our density, and said the thing was all clear and simple to him. But we discovered afterward that he was an escaped lunatic.

The only points of stage "law" on which we are at all clear are as follows:

That if a man dies without leaving a will, then all his property goes to the nearest villain.

But if a man dies and leaves a will, then all his property goes to whoever can get possession of that will.

That the accidental loss of the three-and-sixpenny copy of a marriage certificate annuls the marriage.

That the evidence of one prejudiced witness of shady antecedents is quite sufficient to convict the most stainless and irreproachable gentleman of crimes for the committal of which he could have had no possible motive.

But that this evidence may be rebutted years afterward, and the conviction quashed without further trial by the unsupported statement of the comic man.

That if A forges B's name to a check, then the law of the land is that B shall be sentenced to ten years' penal servitude.

That ten minutes' notice is all that is required to foreclose a mortgage.

That all trials of criminal cases take place in the front parlor of the victim's house, the villain acting as counsel, judge, and jury rolled into one, and a couple of policemen being told off to follow his instructions.

These are a few of the more salient features of stage "law" so far as we have been able to grasp it up to the present; but as fresh acts and clauses and modifications appear to be introduced for each new play, we have abandoned all hope of ever being able to really comprehend the subject.

To return to our hero, the state of the law, as above sketched, naturally confuses him, and the villain, who is the only human being who does seem to understand stage legal questions, is easily able to fleece and ruin him. The simple-minded hero signs mortgages, bills of sale, deeds of gift, and such like things, under the impression that he is playing some sort of a round game; and then when he cannot pay the interest they take his wife and children away from him and turn him adrift into the world.

Being thrown upon his own resources, he naturally starves.

He can make long speeches, he can tell you all his troubles, he can stand in the lime-light and strike attitudes, he can knock the villain down, and he can defy the police, but these requirements are not much in demand in the labor market, and as they are all he can do or cares to do, he finds earning his living a much more difficult affair than he fancied.

There is a deal too much hard work about it for him. He soon gives up trying it at all, and prefers to eke out an uncertain existence by sponging upon good-natured old Irish women and generous but weak-minded young artisans who have left their native village to follow him and enjoy the advantage of his company and conversation.

And so he drags out his life during the middle of the piece, raving at fortune, raging at humanity, and whining about his miseries until the last act.

Then he gets back those "estates" of his into his possession once again, and can go back to the village and make more moral speeches and be happy.

Moral speeches are undoubtedly his leading article, and of these, it must be owned, he has an inexhaustible stock. He is as chock-full of noble sentiments as a bladder is of wind. They are weak and watery sentiments of the sixpenny tea-meeting order. We have a dim notion that we have heard them before. The sound of them always conjures up to our mind the vision of a dull long room, full of oppressive silence, broken only by the scratching of steel pens and an occasional whispered "Give us a suck, Bill. You know I always liked you;" or a louder "Please, sir, speak to Jimmy Boggles. He's a-jogging my elbow."

The stage hero, however, evidently regards these meanderings as gems of brilliant thought, fresh from the philosophic mine.

The gallery greets them with enthusiastic approval. They are a warm-hearted people, galleryites, and they like to give a hearty welcome to old friends.

And then, too, the sentiments are so good and a British gallery is so moral. We doubt if there could be discovered on this earth any body of human beings half so moral--so fond of goodness, even when it is slow and stupid--so hateful of meanness in word or deed--as a modern theatrical gallery.

The early Christian martyrs were sinful and worldly compared with an Adelphi gallery.

The stage hero is a very powerful man. You wouldn't think it to look at him, but you wait till the heroine cries "Help! Oh, George, save me!" or the police attempt to run him in. Then two villains, three extra hired ruffians and four detectives are about his fighting-weight.

If he knocks down less than three men with one blow, he fears that he must be ill, and wonders "Why this strange weakness?"

The hero has his own way of making love. He always does it from behind. The girl turns away from him when he begins (she being, as we have said, shy and timid), and he takes hold of her hands and breathes his attachment down her back.

The stage hero always wears patent-leather boots, and they are always spotlessly clean. Sometimes he is rich and lives in a room with seven doors to it, and at other times he is starving in a garret; but in either event he still wears brand-new patent-leather boots.

He might raise at least three-and-sixpence on those boots, and when the baby is crying for food, it occurs to us that it would be better if, instead of praying to Heaven, he took off those boots and pawned them; but this does not seem to occur to him.

He crosses the African desert in patent-leather boots, does the stage hero. He takes a supply with him when he is wrecked on an uninhabited island. He arrives from long and trying journeys; his clothes are ragged and torn, but his boots are new and shiny. He puts on patent-leather boots to tramp through the Australian bush, to fight in Egypt, to discover the north pole.

Sometimes he is a gold-digger, sometimes a dock laborer, sometimes a soldier, sometimes a sailor, but whatever he is he wears patent-leather boots.

He goes boating in patent leather boots, he plays cricket in them; he goes fishing and shooting in them. He will go to heaven in patent-leather boots or he will decline the invitation.

The stage hero never talks in a simple, straightforward way, like a mere ordinary mortal.

"You will write to me when you are away, dear, won't you?" says the heroine.

A mere human being would reply:

"Why, of course I shall, ducky, every day."

But the stage hero is a superior creature. He says:

"Dost see yonder star, sweet?"

She looks up and owns that she does see yonder star; and then off he starts and drivels on about that star for full five minutes, and says he will cease to write to her when that pale star has fallen from its place amid the firmament of heaven.

The result of a long course of acquaintanceship with stage heroes has been, so far as we are concerned, to create a yearning for a new kind of stage hero. What we would like for a change would be a man who wouldn't cackle and brag quite so much, but who was capable of taking care of himself for a day without getting into trouble.

THE VILLAIN.

He wears a clean collar and smokes a cigarette; that is how we know he is a villain. In real life it is often difficult to tell a villain from an honest man, and this gives rise to mistakes; but on the stage, as we have said villains wear clean collars and smoke cigarettes, and thus all fear of blunder is avoided.

It is well that the rule does not hold off the stage, or good men might be misjudged. We ourselves, for instance, wear a clean collar--sometimes.

It might be very awkward for our family, especially on Sundays.

He has no power of repartee, has the stage villain. All the good people in the play say rude and insulting things to him, and smack at him, and score off him all through the act, but he can never answer them back--can never think of anything clever to say in return.

"Ha! ha! wait till Monday week," is the most brilliant retort that he can make, and he has to get into a corner by himself to think of even that.

The stage villain's career is always very easy and prosperous up to within a minute of the end of each act. Then he gets suddenly let in, generally by the comic man. It always happens so. Yet the villain is always intensely surprised each time. He never seems to learn anything from experience.

A few years ago the villain used to be blessed with a hopeful and philosophical temperament, which enabled him to bear up under these constantly recurring disappointments and reverses. It was "no matter," he would say. Crushed for the moment though he might be, his buoyant heart never lost courage. He had a simple, child-like faith in Providence. "A time will come," he would remark, and this idea consoled him.

Of late, however, this trusting hopefulness of his, as expressed in the beautiful lines we have quoted, appears to have forsaken him. We are sorry for this. We always regarded it as one of the finest traits in his character.

The stage villain's love for the heroine is sublime in its steadfastness. She is a woman of lugubrious and tearful disposition, added to which she is usually incumbered with a couple of priggish and highly objectionable children, and what possible attraction there is about her we ourselves can never understand; but the stage villain--well, there, he is fairly mashed on her.

Nothing can alter his affection. She hates him and insults him to an extent that is really unladylike. Every time he tries to explain his devotion to her, the hero comes in and knocks him down in the middle of it, or the comic man catches him during one or the other of his harassing love-scenes with her, and goes off and tells the "villagers" or the "guests," and they come round and nag him (we should think that the villain must grow to positively dislike the comic man before the piece is over).

Notwithstanding all this he still hankers after her and swears she shall be his. He is not a bad-looking fellow, and from what we know of the market, we should say there are plenty of other girls who would jump at him; yet for the sake of settling down with this dismal young female as his wife, he is prepared to go through a laborious and exhaustive course of crime and to be bullied and insulted by every one he meets. His love sustains him under it all. He robs and forges, and cheats, and lies, and murders, and arsons. If there were any other crimes he could commit to win her affection, he would, for her sweet sake, commit them cheerfully. But he doesn't know any others--at all events, he is not well up in any others--and she still does not care for him, and what is he to do?

It is very unfortunate for both of them. It is evident to the merest spectator that the lady's life would be much happier if the villain did not love her quite so much; and as for him, his career might be calmer and less criminal but for his deep devotion to her.

You see, it is having met her in early life that is the cause of all the trouble. He first saw her when she was a child, and he loved her, "ay, even then." Ah, and he would have worked--slaved for her, and have made her rich and happy. He might perhaps even have been a good man.

She tries to soothe him. She says she loathed him with an unspeakable horror from the first moment that her eyes met his revolting form. She says she saw a hideous toad once in a nasty pond, and she says that rather would she take that noisome reptile and clasp its slimy bosom to her own than tolerate one instant's touch from his (the villain's) arms.

This sweet prattle of hers, however, only charms him all the more. He says he will win her yet.

Nor does the villain seem much happier in his less serious love episodes. After he has indulged in a little badinage of the above character with his real lady-love, the heroine, he will occasionally try a little light flirtation passage with her maid or lady friend.

The maid or friend does not waste time in simile or in metaphor. She calls him a black-hearted scoundrel and clumps him over the head.

Of recent years it has been attempted to cheer the stage villain's loveless life by making the village clergyman's daughter gone on him. But it is generally about ten years ago when even she loved him, and her love has turned to hate by the time the play opens; so that on the whole his lot can hardly be said to have been much improved in this direction.

Not but what it must be confessed that her change of feeling is, under the circumstances, only natural. He took her away from her happy, peaceful home when she was very young and brought her up to this wicked overgrown London. He did not marry her. There is no earthly reason why he should not have married her. She must have been a fine girl at that time (and she is a good-looking woman as it is, with dash and go about her), and any other man would have settled down cozily with her and have led a simple, blameless life.

But the stage villain is built cussed.

He ill-uses this female most shockingly--not for any cause or motive whatever; indeed, his own practical interests should prompt him to treat her well and keep friends with her--but from the natural cussedness to which we have just alluded. When he speaks to her he seizes her by the wrist and breathes what he's got to say into her ear, and it tickles and revolts her.

The only thing in which he is good to her is in the matter of dress. He does not stint her in dress.

The stage villain is superior to the villain of real life. The villain of real life is actuated by mere sordid and selfish motives. The stage villain does villainy, not for any personal advantage to himself, but merely from the love of the thing as an art. Villainy is to him its own reward; he revels in it.

"Better far be poor and villainous," he says to himself, "than possess all the wealth of the Indies with a clear conscience. I will be a villain," he cries. "I will, at great expense and inconvenience to myself, murder the good old man, get the hero accused of the crime, and make love to his wife while he is in prison. It will be a risky and laborious business for me from beginning to end, and can bring me no practical advantage whatever. The girl will call me insulting names when I pay her a visit, and will push me violently in the chest when I get near her; her golden-haired infant will say I am a bad man and may even refuse to kiss me. The comic man will cover me with humorous opprobrium, and the villagers will get a day off and hang about the village pub and hoot me. Everybody will see through my villainy, and I shall be nabbed in the end. I always am. But it is no matter, I will be a villain--ha! ha!"

On the whole, the stage villain appears to us to be a rather badly used individual. He never has any "estates" or property himself, and his only chance of getting on in the world is to sneak the hero's. He has an affectionate disposition, and never having any wife of his own he is compelled to love other people's; but his affection is ever unrequited, and everything comes wrong for him in the end.

Our advice to stage villains generally, after careful observation of (stage) life and (stage) human nature, is as follows:

Never be a stage villain at all if you can help it. The life is too harassing and the remuneration altogether disproportionate to the risks and labor.

If you have run away with the clergyman's daughter and she still clings to you, do not throw her down in the center of the stage and call her names. It only irritates her, and she takes a dislike to you and goes and warns the other girl.

Don't have too many accomplices; and if you have got them, don't keep sneering at them and bullying them. A word from them can hang you, and yet you do all you can to rile them. Treat them civilly and let them have their fair share of the swag.

Beware of the comic man. When you are committing a murder or robbing a safe you never look to see where the comic man is. You are so careless in that way. On the whole, it might be as well if you murdered the comic man early in the play.

Don't make love to the hero's wife. She doesn't like you; how can you expect her to? Besides, it isn't proper. Why don't you get a girl of your own?

Lastly, don't go down to the scenes of your crimes in the last act. You always will do this. We suppose it is some extra cheap excursion down there that attracts you. But take our advice and don't go. That is always where you get nabbed. The police know your habits from experience. They do not trouble to look for you. They go down in the last act to the old hall or the ruined mill where you did the deed and wait for you.

In nine cases out of ten you would get off scot-free but for this idiotic custom of yours. Do keep away from the place. Go abroad or to the sea-side when the last act begins and stop there till it is over. You will be safe then.

THE HEROINE.

She is always in trouble--and don't she let you know it, too! Her life is undeniably a hard one. Nothing goes right with her. We all have our troubles, but the stage heroine never has anything else. If she only got one afternoon a week off from trouble or had her Sundays free it would be something.

But no; misfortune stalks beside her from week's beginning to week's end.

After her husband has been found guilty of murder, which is about the least thing that can ever happen to him, and her white-haired father has become a bankrupt and has died of a broken heart, and the home of her childhood has been sold up, then her infant goes and contracts a lingering fever.

She weeps a good deal during the course of her troubles, which we suppose is only natural enough, poor woman. But it is depressing from the point of view of the audience, and we almost wish before the evening is out that she had not got quite so much trouble.

It is over the child that she does most of her weeping. The child has a damp time of it altogether. We sometimes wonder that it never catches rheumatism.

She is very good, is the stage heroine. The comic man expresses a belief that she is a born angel. She reproves him for this with a tearful smile (it wouldn't be her smile if it wasn't tearful).

"Oh, no," she says (sadly of course); "I have many, many faults."

We rather wish that she would show them a little more. Her excessive goodness seems somehow to pall upon us. Our only consolation while watching her is that there are not many good women off the stage. Life is bad enough as it is; if there were many women in real life as good as the stage heroine, it would be unbearable.

The stage heroine's only pleasure in life is to go out in a snow-storm without an umbrella and with no bonnet on. She has a bonnet, we know (rather a tasteful little thing); we have seen it hanging up behind the door of her room; but when she comes out for a night stroll during a heavy snow-storm (accompanied by thunder), she is most careful to leave it at home. Maybe she fears the snow will spoil it, and she is a careful girl.

She always brings her child out with her on these occasions. She seems to think that it will freshen it up. The child does not appreciate the snow as much as she does. He says it's cold.

One thing that must irritate the stage heroine very much on these occasions is the way in which the snow seems to lie in wait for her and follow her about. It is quite a fine night before she comes on the scene: the moment she appears it begins to snow. It snows heavily all the while she remains about, and the instant she goes it clears up again and keeps dry for the rest of the evening.

The way the snow "goes" for that poor woman is most unfair. It always snows much heavier in the particular spot where she is sitting than it does anywhere else in the whole street. Why, we have sometimes seen a heroine sitting in the midst of a blinding snow-storm while the other side of the road was as dry as a bone. And it never seemed to occur to her to cross over.

We have even known a more than unusually malignant snow-storm to follow a heroine three times round the stage and then go off (R.) with her.

Of course you can't get away from a snow-storm like that! A stage snow-storm is the kind of snow-storm that would follow you upstairs and want to come into bed with you.

Another curious thing about these stage snow-storms is that the moon is always shining brightly through the whole of them. And it shines only on the heroine, and it follows her about just like the snow does.

Nobody fully understands what a wonderful work of nature the moon is except people acquainted with the stage. Astronomy teaches you something about the moon, but you learn a good deal more from a few visits to a theater. You will find from the latter that the moon only shines on heroes and heroines, with perhaps an occasional beam on the comic man: it always goes out when it sees the villain coming.

It is surprising, too, how quickly the moon can go out on the stage. At one moment it is riding in full radiance in the midst of a cloudless sky, and the next instant it is gone! Just as though it had been turned off at a meter. It makes you quite giddy at first until you get used to it.

The stage heroine is inclined to thoughtfulness rather than gayety.

In her cheerful moments the stage heroine thinks she sees the spirit of her mother, or the ghost of her father, or she dreams of her dead baby.

But this is only in her very merry moods. As a rule, she is too much occupied with weeping to have time for frivolous reflections.

She has a great flow of language and a wonderful gift of metaphor and simile--more forcible than elegant--and this might be rather trying in a wife under ordinary circumstances. But as the hero is generally sentenced to ten years' penal servitude on his wedding-morn, he escapes for a period from a danger that might well appall a less fortunate bridegroom.

Sometimes the stage heroine has a brother, and if so he is sure to be mistaken for her lover. We never came across a brother and sister in real life who ever gave the most suspicious person any grounds for mistaking them for lovers; but the stage brother and sister are so affectionate that the error is excusable.

And when the mistake does occur and the husband comes in suddenly and finds them kissing and raves she doesn't turn round and say:

"Why, you silly cuckoo, it's only my brother."

That would be simple and sensible, and would not suit the stage heroine at all. No; she does all in her power to make everybody believe it is true, so that she can suffer in silence.

She does so love to suffer.

Marriage is undoubtedly a failure in the case of the stage heroine.

If the stage heroine were well advised she would remain single. Her husband means well. He is decidedly affectionate. But he is unfortunate and inexperienced in worldly affairs. Things come right for him at the end of the play, it is true; but we would not recommend the heroine to place too much reliance upon the continuance of this happy state of affairs. From what we have seen of her husband and his business capabilities during the five acts preceding, we are inclined to doubt the possibility of his being anything but unfortunate to the end of his career.

True, he has at last got his "rights" (which he would never have lost had he had a head instead of a sentimental bladder on his shoulders), the Villain is handcuffed, and he and the heroine have settled down comfortably next door to the comic man.

But this heavenly existence will never last. The stage hero was built for trouble, and he will be in it again in another month, you bet. They'll get up another mortgage for him on the "estates;" and he won't know, bless you, whether he really did sign it or whether he didn't, and out he will go.

And he'll slop his name about to documents without ever looking to see what he's doing, and be let in for Lord knows what; and another wife will turn up for him that he had married when a boy and forgotten all about.

And the next corpse that comes to the village he'll get mixed up with--sure to--and have it laid to his door, and there'll be all the old business over again.

No, our advice to the stage heroine is to get rid of the hero as soon as possible, marry the villain, and go and live abroad somewhere where the comic man won't come fooling around.

She will be much happier.

THE COMIC MAN.

He follows the hero all over the world. This is rough on the hero.

What makes him so gone on the hero is that when they were boys together the hero used to knock him down and kick him. The comic man remembers this with a glow of pride when he is grown up, and it makes him love the hero and determine to devote his life to him.

He is a man of humble station--the comic man. The village blacksmith or a peddler. You never see a rich or aristocratic comic man on the stage. You can have your choice on the stage; you can be funny and of lowly origin, or you can be well-to-do and without any sense of humor. Peers and policemen are the people most utterly devoid of humor on the stage.

The chief duty of the comic man's life is to make love to servant-girls, and they slap his face; but it does not discourage him; he seems to be more smitten by them than ever.

The comic man is happy under any fate, and he says funny things at funerals and when the bailiffs are in the house or the hero is waiting to be hanged.

This sort of man is rather trying in real life. In real life such a man would probably be slaughtered to death and buried at an early period of his career, but on the stage they put up with him.

He is very good, is the comic man. He can't bear villainy. To thwart villainy is his life's ambition, and in this noble object fortune backs him up grandly. Bad people come and commit their murders and thefts right under his nose, so that he can denounce them in the last act.

They never see him there, standing close beside them, while they are performing these fearful crimes.

It is marvelous how short-sighted people on the stage are. We always thought that the young lady in real life was moderately good at not seeing folks she did not want to when they were standing straight in front of her, but her affliction in this direction is as nothing compared with that of her brothers and sisters on the stage.

These unfortunate people come into rooms where there are crowds of people about--people that it is most important that they should see, and owing to not seeing whom they get themselves into fearful trouble, and they never notice any of them. They talk to somebody opposite, and they can't see a third person that is standing bang between the two of them.

You might fancy they wore blinkers.

Then, again, their hearing is so terribly weak. It really ought to be seen to. People talk and chatter at the very top of their voices close behind them, and they never hear a word--don't know anybody's there, even. After it has been going on for half an hour, and the people "up stage" have made themselves hoarse with shouting, and somebody has been boisterously murdered and all the furniture upset, then the people "down stage" "think they hear a noise."

The comic man always rows with his wife if he is married or with his sweetheart if he is not married. They quarrel all day long. It must be a trying life, you would think, but they appear to like it.

How the comic man lives and supports his wife (she looks as if it wanted something to support her, too) and family is always a mystery to us. As we have said, he is not a rich man and he never seems to earn any money. Sometimes he keeps a shop, and in the way he manages business it must be an expensive thing to keep, for he never charges anybody for anything, he is so generous. All his customers seem to be people more or less in trouble, and he can't find it in his heart to ask them to pay for their goods under such distressing circumstances.

He stuffs their basket full with twice as much as they came to buy, pushes their money back into their hands, and wipes away a tear.

Why doesn't a comic man come and set up a grocery store in our neighborhood?

When the shop does not prove sufficiently profitable (as under the above-explained method sometimes happens to be the case) the comic man's wife seeks to add to the income by taking in lodgers. This is a bad move on her part, for it always ends in the lodgers taking her in. The hero and heroine, who seem to have been waiting for something of the sort, immediately come and take possession of the whole house.

Of course the comic man could not think of charging for mere board and lodging the man who knocked him down when they were boys together! Besides, was not the heroine (now the hero's wife) the sweetest and the blithest girl in all the village of Deepdale? (They must have been a gloomy band, the others!) How can any one with a human heart beneath his bosom suggest that people like that should pay for their rest and washing? The comic man is shocked at his wife for even thinking of such a thing, and the end of it is that Mr. and Mrs. Hero live there for the rest of the play rent free; coals, soap, candles, and hair-oil for the child being provided for them on the same terms.

The hero raises vague and feeble objections to this arrangement now and again. He says he will not hear of such a thing, that he will stay no longer to be a burden upon these honest folk, but will go forth unto the roadside and there starve. The comic man has awful work with him, but wins at last and persuades the noble fellow to stop on and give the place another trial.

When, a morning or so after witnessing one of these beautiful scenes, our own landlady knocks at our door and creates a disturbance over a paltry matter of three or four weeks' rent, and says she'll have her money or out we go that very day, and drifts slowly away down toward the kitchen, abusing us in a rising voice as she descends, then we think of these things and grow sad.

It is the example of the people round him that makes the comic man so generous. Everybody is generous on the stage. They are giving away their purses all day long; that is the regulation "tip" on the stage--one's purse. The moment you hear a tale of woe, you grab it out of your pocket, slap it in to the woe-er's palm, grip his hand, dash away a tear, and exit; you don't even leave yourself a 'bus fare home. You walk back quickly and get another purse.

Middle-class people and others on the stage who are short of purses have to content themselves with throwing about rolls of bank-notes and tipping servants with five-pound checks. Very stingy people on the stage have been known to be so cussed mean as to give away mere sovereigns.

But they are generally only villains or lords that descend to this sort of thing. Respectable stage folk never offer anything less than a purse.

The recipient is very grateful on receiving the purse (he never looks inside) and thinks that Heaven ought to reward the donor. They get a lot of work out of Heaven on the stage. Heaven does all the odd jobs for them that they don't want to go to the trouble and expense of doing for themselves. Heaven's chief duty on the stage is to see to the repayment of all those sums of money that are given or lent to the good people. It is generally requested to do this to the tune of a "thousand-fold"--an exorbitant rate when you come to think of it.

Heaven is also expected to take care that the villain gets properly cursed, and to fill up its spare time by bringing misfortune upon the local landlord. It has to avenge everybody and to help all the good people whenever they are in trouble. And they keep it going in this direction.

And when the hero leaves for prison Heaven has to take care of his wife and child till he comes out; and if this isn't a handful for it, we don't know what would be!

Heaven on the stage is always on the side of the hero and heroine and against the police.

Occasionally, of late years, the comic man has been a bad man, but you can't hate him for it. What if he does ruin the hero and rob the heroine and help to murder the good old man? He does it all in such a genial, light-hearted spirit that it is not in one's heart to feel angry with him. It is the way in which a thing is done that makes all the difference.

Besides, he can always round on his pal, the serious villain, at the end, and that makes it all right.

The comic man is not a sportsman. If he goes out shooting, we know that when he returns we shall hear that he has shot the dog. If he takes his girl out on the river he upsets her (literally we mean). The comic man never goes out for a day's pleasure without coming home a wreck.

If he merely goes to tea with his girl at her mother's, he swallows a muffin and chokes himself.

The comic man is not happy in his married life, nor does it seem to us that he goes the right way to be so. He calls his wife "his old Dutch clock," "the old geyser," and such like terms of endearment, and addresses her with such remarks as "Ah, you old cat," "You ugly old nutmeg grater," "You orangamatang, you!" etc., etc.

Well, you know that is not the way to make things pleasant about a house.

Still, with all his faults we like the comic man. He is not always in trouble and he does not make long speeches.

Let us bless him.

THE LAWYER.

He is very old, and very long, and very thin. He has white hair. He dresses in the costume of the last generation but seven. He has bushy eyebrows and is clean shaven. His chin itches considerably, so that he has to be always scratching it. His favorite remark is "Ah!"

In real life we have heard of young solicitors, of foppish solicitors, of short solicitors; but on the stage they are always very thin and very old. The youngest stage solicitor we ever remember to have seen looked about sixty--the oldest about a hundred and forty-five.

By the bye, it is never very safe to judge people's ages on the stage by their personal appearance. We have known old ladies who looked seventy, if they were a day, turn out to be the mothers of boys of fourteen, while the middle-aged husband of the young wife generally gives one the idea of ninety.

Again, what appears at first sight to be a comfortable-looking and eminently respectable elderly lady is often discovered to be, in reality, a giddy, girlish, and inexperienced young thing, the pride of the village or the darling of the regiment.

So, too, an exceptionally stout and short-winded old gentleman, who looks as if he had been living too well and taking too little exercise for the last forty-five years, is not the heavy father, as you might imagine if you judged from mere external evidence, but a wild, reckless boy.

You would not think so to look at him, but his only faults are that he is so young and light-headed. There is good in him, however, and he will no doubt be steady enough when he grows up. All the young men of the neighborhood worship him and the girls love him.

"Here he comes," they say; "dear, dear old Jack--Jack, the darling boy--the headstrong youth--Jack, the leader of our juvenile sports--Jack, whose childish innocence wins all hearts. Three cheers for dancing, bright-eyed Jack!"

On the other hand, ladies with the complexion of eighteen are, you learn as the story progresses, quite elderly women, the mothers of middle-aged heroes.

The experienced observer of stage-land never jumps to conclusions from what he sees. He waits till he is told things.

The stage lawyer never has any office of his own. He transacts all his business at his clients' houses. He will travel hundreds of miles to tell them the most trivial piece of legal information.

It never occurs to him how much simpler it would be to write a letter. The item for "traveling expenses" in his bill of costs must be something enormous.

There are two moments in the course of his client's career that the stage lawyer particularly enjoys. The first is when the client comes unexpectedly into a fortune; the second when he unexpectedly loses it.

In the former case, upon learning the good news the stage lawyer at once leaves his business and hurries off to the other end of the kingdom to bear the glad tidings. He arrives at the humble domicile of the beneficiary in question, sends up his card, and is ushered into the front parlor. He enters mysteriously and sits left--client sits right. An ordinary, common lawyer would come to the point at once, state the matter in a plain, business-like way, and trust that he might have the pleasure of representing, etc., etc.; but such simple methods are not those of the stage lawyer. He looks at the client and says:

"You had a father."

The client starts. How on earth did this calm, thin, keen-eyed old man in black know that he had a father? He shuffles and stammers, but the quiet, impenetrable lawyer fixes his cold, glassy eye on him, and he is helpless. Subterfuge, he feels, is useless, and amazed, bewildered at the knowledge of his most private affairs possessed by his strange visitant, he admits the fact: he had a father.

The lawyer smiles with a quiet smile of triumph and scratches his chin.

"You had a mother, too, if I am informed correctly," he continues.

It is idle attempting to escape this man's supernatural acuteness, and the client owns up to having had a mother also.

From this the lawyer goes on to communicate to the client, as a great secret, the whole of his (the client's) history from his cradle upward, and also the history of his nearer relatives, and in less than half an hour from the old man's entrance, or say forty minutes at the outside, the client almost knows what the business is about.

On the other occasion, when the client has lost his fortune, the stage lawyer is even still happier. He comes down himself to tell the misfortune (he would not miss the job for worlds), and he takes care to choose the most unpropitious moment possible for breaking the news. On the eldest daughter's birthday, when there is a big party on, is his favorite time. He comes in about midnight and tells them just as they are going down to supper.

He has no idea of business hours, has the stage lawyer--to make the thing as unpleasant as possible seems to be his only anxiety.

If he cannot work it for a birthday, then he waits till there's a wedding on, and gets up early in the morning on purpose to run down and spoil the show. To enter among a crowd of happy, joyous fellow-creatures and leave them utterly crushed and miserable is the stage lawyer's hobby.

The stage lawyer is a very talkative gentleman. He regards the telling of his client's most private affairs to every stranger that he meets as part of his professional duties. A good gossip with a few chance acquaintances about the family secrets of his employers is food and drink for the stage lawyer.

They all go about telling their own and their friends' secrets to perfect strangers on the stage. Whenever two people have five minutes to spare on the stage they tell each other the story of their lives. "Sit down and I will tell you the story of my life" is the stage equivalent for the "Come and have a drink" of the outside world.

The good stage lawyer has generally nursed the heroine on his knee when a baby (when she was a baby, we mean)--when she was only so high. It seems to have been a part of his professional duties. The good stage lawyer also kisses all the pretty girls in the play and is expected to chuck the housemaid under the chin. It is good to be a good stage lawyer.

The good stage lawyer also wipes away a tear when sad things happen; and he turns away to do this and blows his nose, and says he thinks he has a fly in his eye. This touching trait in his character is always held in great esteem by the audience and is much applauded.

The good stage lawyer is never by any chance a married man. (Few good men are, so we gather from our married lady friends.) He loved in early life the heroine's mother. That "sainted woman" (tear and nose business) died and is now among the angels--the gentleman who did marry her, by the bye, is not quite so sure about this latter point, but the lawyer is fixed on the idea.

In stage literature of a frivolous nature the lawyer is a very different individual. In comedy he is young, he possesses chambers, and he is married (there is no doubt about this latter fact); and his wife and his mother-in-law spend most of the day in his office and make the dull old place quite lively for him.

He only has one client. She is a nice lady and affable, but her antecedents are doubtful, and she seems to be no better than she ought to be--possibly worse. But anyhow she is the sole business that the poor fellow has--is, in fact, his only source of income, and might, one would think, under such circumstances be accorded a welcome by his family. But his wife and his mother-in-law, on the contrary, take a violent dislike to her, and the lawyer has to put her in the coal-scuttle or lock her up in the safe whenever he hears either of these female relatives of his coming up the stairs.

We should not care to be the client of a farcical comedy stage lawyer. Legal transactions are trying to the nerves under the most favorable circumstances; conducted by a farcical stage lawyer, the business would be too exciting for us.

THE ADVENTURESS.

She sits on a table and smokes a cigarette. A cigarette on the stage is always the badge of infamy.

In real life the cigarette is usually the hall-mark of the particularly mild and harmless individual. It is the dissipation of the Y.M.C.A.; the innocent joy of the pure-hearted boy long ere the demoralizing influence of our vaunted civilization has dragged him down into the depths of the short clay.

But behind the cigarette on the stage lurks ever black-hearted villainy and abandoned womanhood.

The adventuress is generally of foreign extraction. They do not make bad women in England--the article is entirely of continental manufacture and has to be imported. She speaks English with a charming little French accent, and she makes up for this by speaking French with a good sound English one.

She seems a smart business woman, and she would probably get on very well if it were not for her friends and relations. Friends and relations are a trying class of people even in real life, as we all know, but the friends and relations of the stage adventuress are a particularly irritating lot. They never leave her; never does she get a day or an hour off from them. Wherever she goes, there the whole tribe goes with her.

They all go with her in a body when she calls on her young man, and it is as much as she can do to persuade them to go into the next room even for five minutes, and give her a chance. When she is married they come and live with her.

They know her dreadful secret and it keeps them in comfort for years. Knowing somebody's secret seems, on the stage, to be one of the most profitable and least exhausting professions going.

She is fond of married life, is the adventuress, and she goes in for it pretty extensively. She has husbands all over the globe, most of them in prison, but they escape and turn up in the last act and spoil all the poor girl's plans. That is so like husbands--no consideration, no thought for their poor wives. They are not a prepossessing lot, either, those early husbands of hers. What she could have seen in them to induce her to marry them is indeed a mystery.

The adventuress dresses magnificently. Where she gets the money from we never could understand, for she and her companions are always more or less complaining of being "stone broke." Dressmakers must be a trusting people where she comes from.

The adventuress is like the proverbial cat as regards the number of lives she is possessed of. You never know when she is really dead. Most people like to die once and have done with it, but the adventuress, after once or twice trying it, seems to get quite to like it, and goes on giving way to it, and then it grows upon her until she can't help herself, and it becomes a sort of craving with her.

This habit of hers is, however, a very trying one for her friends and husbands--it makes things so uncertain. Something ought to be done to break her of it. Her husbands, on hearing that she is dead, go into raptures and rush off and marry other people, and then just as they are starting off on their new honeymoon up she crops again, as fresh as paint. It is really most annoying.

For ourselves, were we the husband of a stage adventuress we should never, after what we have seen of the species, feel quite justified in believing her to be dead unless we had killed and buried her ourselves; and even then we should be more easy in our minds if we could arrange to sit on her grave for a week or so afterward. These women are so artful!

But it is not only the adventuress who will persist in coming to life again every time she is slaughtered. They all do it on the stage. They are all so unreliable in this respect. It must be most disheartening to the murderers.

And then, again, it is something extraordinary, when you come to think of it, what a tremendous amount of killing some of them can stand and still come up smiling in the next act, not a penny the worse for it. They get stabbed, and shot, and thrown over precipices thousands of feet high and, bless you, it does them good--it is like a tonic to them.

As for the young man that is coming home to see his girl, you simply can't kill him. Achilles was a summer rose compared with him. Nature and mankind have not sufficient materials in hand as yet to kill that man. Science has but the strength of a puling babe against his invulnerability. You can waste your time on earthquakes and shipwrecks, volcanic eruptions, floods, explosions, railway accidents, and such like sort of things, if you are foolish enough to do so; but it is no good your imagining that anything of the kind can hurt him, because it can't.

There will be thousands of people killed, thousands in each instance, but one human being will always escape, and that one human being will be the stage young man who is coming home to see his girl.

He is forever being reported as dead, but it always turns out to be another fellow who was like him or who had on his (the young man's) hat. He is bound to be out of it, whoever else may be in.

"If I had been at my post that day," he explains to his sobbing mother, "I should have been blown up, but the Providence that watches over good men had ordained that I should be laying blind drunk in Blogg's saloon at the time the explosion took place, and so the other engineer, who had been doing my work when it was his turn to be off, was killed along with the whole of the crew."

"Ah, thank Heaven, thank Heaven for that!" ejaculates the pious old lady, and the comic man is so overcome with devout joy that he has to relieve his overstrained heart by drawing his young woman on one side and grossly insulting her.

All attempts to kill this young man ought really to be given up now. The job has been tried over and over again by villains and bad people of all kinds, but no one has ever succeeded. There has been an amount of energy and ingenuity expended in seeking to lay up that one man which, properly utilized, might have finished off ten million ordinary mortals. It is sad to think of so much wasted effort.

He, the young man coming home to see his girl, need never take an insurance ticket or even buy a *Tit Bits*. It would be needless expenditure in his case.

On the other hand, and to make matters equal, as it were, there are some stage people so delicate that it is next door to impossible to keep them alive.

The inconvenient husband is a most pathetic example of this. Medical science is powerless to save that man when the last act comes round; indeed, we doubt whether medical science, in its present state of development, could even tell what is the matter with him or why he dies at all. He looks healthy and robust enough and nobody touches him, yet down he drops, without a word of warning, stone-dead, in the middle of the floor--he always dies in the middle of the floor. Some folks like to die in bed, but stage people don't. They like to die on the floor. We all have our different tastes.

The adventuress herself is another person who dies with remarkable ease. We suppose in her case it is being so used to it that makes her so quick and clever at it. There is no lingering illness and doctors' bills and upsetting of the whole household arrangements about her method. One walk round the stage and the thing is done.

All bad characters die quickly on the stage. Good characters take a long time over it, and have a sofa down in the drawing-room to do it on, and have sobbing relatives and good old doctors fooling around them, and can smile and forgive everybody. Bad stage characters have to do the whole job, dying speech and all, in about ten seconds, and do it with all their clothes on into the bargain, which must make it most uncomfortable.

It is repentance that kills off the bad people in plays. They always repent, and the moment they repent they die. Repentance on the stage seems to be one of the most dangerous things a man can be taken with. Our advice to stage wicked people would undoubtedly be, "Never repent. If you value your life, don't repent. It always means sudden death!"

To return to our adventuress. She is by no means a bad woman. There is much good in her. This is more than proved by the fact that she learns to love the hero before she dies; for no one but a really good woman capable of extraordinary patience and gentleness could ever, we are convinced, grow to feel any other sentiment for that irritating ass, than a desire to throw bricks at him.

The stage adventuress would be a much better woman, too, if it were not for the heroine. The adventuress makes the most complete arrangements for being noble and self-sacrificing--that is, for going away and never coming back, and is just about to carry them out, when the heroine, who has a perfect genius for being in the wrong place at the right time, comes in and spoils it all. No stage adventuress can be good while the heroine is about. The sight of the heroine rouses every bad feeling in her breast.

We can sympathize with her in this respect. The heroine often affects ourselves in precisely the same way.

There is a good deal to be said in favor of the adventuress. True, she possesses rather too much sarcasm and repartee to make things quite agreeable round the domestic hearth, and when she has got all her clothes on there is not much room left in the place for anybody else; but taken on the whole she is decidedly attractive. She has grit and go in her. She is alive. She can do something to help herself besides calling for "George."

She has not got a stage child--if she ever had one, she has left it on somebody else's doorstep which, presuming there was no water handy to drown it in, seems to be about the most sensible thing she could have done with it. She is not oppressively good.

She never wants to be "unhanded" or "let to pass."

She is not always being shocked or insulted by people telling her that they love her; she does not seem to mind it if they do. She is not always fainting, and crying, and sobbing, and wailing, and moaning, like the good people in the play are.

Oh, they do have an unhappy time of it--the good people in plays! Then she is the only person in the piece who can sit on the comic man.

We sometimes think it would be a fortunate thing--for him--if they allowed her to marry and settle down quietly with the hero. She might make a man of him in time.

THE SERVANT-GIRL.

There are two types of servant-girl to be met with on the stage. This is an unusual allowance for one profession.

There is the lodging-house slavey. She has a good heart and a smutty face and is always dressed according to the latest fashion in scarecrows. Her leading occupation is the cleaning of boots. She cleans boots all over the house, at all hours of the day. She comes and sits down on the hero's breakfast-table and cleans them over the poor fellow's food. She comes into the drawing-room cleaning boots.

She has her own method of cleaning them, too. She rubs off the mud, puts on the blacking, and polishes up all with the same brush. They take an enormous amount of polishing. She seems to do nothing else all day long but walk about shining one boot, and she breathes on it and rubs it till you wonder there is any leather left, yet it never seems to get any brighter, nor, indeed, can you expect it to, for when you look close you see it is a patent-leather boot that she has been throwing herself away upon all this time.

Somebody has been having a lark with the poor girl.

The lodging-house slavey brushes her hair with the boot brush and blacks the end of her nose with it.

We were acquainted with a lodging-house slavey once--a real one, we mean. She was the handmaiden at a house in Bloomsbury where we once hung out. She was untidy in her dress, it is true, but she had not quite that castaway and gone-to-sleep-in-a-dust-bin appearance that we, an earnest student of the drama, felt she ought to present, and we questioned her one day on the subject.

"How is it, Sophronia," we said, "that you distantly resemble a human being instead of giving one the idea of an animated rag-shop? Don't you ever polish your nose with the blacking-brush, or rub coal into your head, or wash your face in treacle, or put skewers into your hair, or anything of that sort, like they do on the stage?"

She said: "Lord love you, what should I want to go and be a bally idiot like that for?"

And we have not liked to put the question elsewhere since then.

The other type of servant-girl on the stage--the villa servant-girl--is a very different personage. She is a fetching little thing, dresses bewitchingly, and is always clean. Her duties are to dust the legs of the chairs in the drawing-room. That is the only work she ever has to do, but it must be confessed she does that thoroughly. She never comes into the room without dusting the legs of these chairs, and she dusts them again before she goes out.

If anything ought to be free from dust in a stage house, it should be the legs of the drawing-room chairs.

She is going to marry the man-servant, is the stage servant-girl, as soon as they have saved up sufficient out of their wages to buy a hotel. They think they will like to keep a hotel. They don't understand a bit about the business, which we believe is a complicated one, but this does not trouble them in the least.

They quarrel a good deal over their love-making, do the stage servant-girl and her young man, and they always come into the drawing-room to do it. They have got the kitchen, and there is the garden (with a fountain and mountains in the background--you can see it through the window), but no! no place in or about the house is good enough for them to quarrel in except the drawing-room. They quarrel there so vigorously that it even interferes with the dusting of the chair-legs.

She ought not to be long in saving up sufficient to marry on, for the generosity of people on the stage to the servants there makes one seriously consider the advisability of ignoring the unremunerative professions of ordinary life and starting a new and more promising career as a stage servant.

No one ever dreams of tipping the stage servant with less than a sovereign when they ask her if her mistress is at home or give her a letter to post, and there is quite a rush at the end of the piece to stuff five-pound notes into her hand. The good old man gives her ten.

The stage servant is very impudent to her mistress, and the master--he falls in love with her and it does upset the house so.

Sometimes the servant-girl is good and faithful, and then she is Irish. All good servant-girls on the stage are Irish.

All the male visitors are expected to kiss the stage servant-girl when they come into the house, and to dig her in the ribs and to say: "Do you know, Jane, I think you're an uncommonly nice girl--click." They always say this, and she likes it.

Many years ago, when we were young, we thought we would see if things were the same off the stage, and the next time we called at a certain friend's house we tried this business on.

She wasn't quite so dazzlingly beautiful as they are on the stage, but we passed that. She showed us up into the drawing-room, and then said she would go and tell her mistress we were there.

We felt this was the time to begin. We skipped between her and the door. We held our hat in front of us, cocked our head on one side, and said: "Don't go! don't go!"

The girl seemed alarmed. We began to get a little nervous ourselves, but we had begun it and we meant to go through with it.

We said, "Do you know, Jane" (her name wasn't Jane, but that wasn't our fault), "do you know, Jane, I think you're an uncommonly nice girl," and we said "click," and dug her in the ribs with our elbow, and then chucked her under the chin. The whole thing seemed to fall flat. There was nobody there to laugh or applaud. We wished we hadn't done it. It seemed stupid when you came to think of it. We began to feel frightened. The business wasn't going as we expected; but we screwed up our courage and went on.

We put on the customary expression of comic imbecility and beckoned the girl to us. We have never seen this fail on the stage.

But this girl seemed made wrong. She got behind the sofa and screamed "Help!"

We have never known them to do this on the stage, and it threw us out in our plans. We did not know exactly what to do. We regretted that we had ever begun this job and heartily wished ourselves out of it. But it appeared foolish to pause then, when we were more than half-way through, and we made a rush to get it over.

We chivvied the girl round the sofa and caught her near the door and kissed her.

She scratched our face, yelled police, murder, and fire, and fled from the room.

Our friend came in almost immediately. He said:

"I say, J., old man, are you drunk?"

We told him no, that we were only a student of the drama. His wife then entered in a towering passion. She didn't ask us if we were drunk. She said:

"How dare you come here in this state!"

We endeavored unsuccessfully to induce her to believe that we were sober, and we explained that our course of conduct was what was always pursued on the stage.

She said she didn't care what was done on the stage, it wasn't going to be pursued in her house; and that if her husband's friends couldn't behave as gentlemen they had better stop away.

The following morning we received a letter from a firm of solicitors in Lincoln's Inn with reference, so they put it, to the brutal and unprovoked assault committed by us on the previous afternoon upon the person of their client, Miss Matilda Hemmings. The letter stated that we had punched Miss Hemmings in the side, struck her under the chin, and afterward, seizing her as she was leaving the room, proceeded to commit a gross assault, into the particulars of which it was needless for them to enter at greater length.

It added that if we were prepared to render an ample written apology and to pay 50 pounds compensation, they would advise their client, Miss Matilda Hemmings, to allow the matter to drop; otherwise criminal proceedings would at once be commenced against us.

We took the letter to our own solicitors and explained the circumstances to them. They said it seemed to be a very sad case, but advised us to pay the 50 pounds, and we borrowed the money and did so.

Since then we have lost faith, somehow, in the British drama as a guide to the conduct of life.

THE CHILD.

It is nice and quiet and it talks prettily.

We have come across real infants now and then in the course of visits to married friends; they have been brought to us from outlying parts of the house and introduced to us for our edification; and we have found them gritty and sticky. Their boots have usually been muddy, and they have wiped them up against our new trousers. And their hair has suggested the idea that they have been standing on their heads in the dust-bin.

And they have talked to us--but not prettily, not at all--rather rude we should call it.

But the stage child is very different. It is clean and tidy. You can touch it anywhere and nothing comes off. Its face glows with soap and water. From the appearance of its hands it is evident that mud-pies and tar are joys unknown to it. As for its hair, there is something uncanny about its smoothness and respectability. Even its boot-laces are done up.

We have never seen anything like the stage child outside a theater excepting one--that was on the pavement in front of a tailor's shop in Tottenham Court Road. He stood on a bit of round wood, and it was fifteen and nine, his style.

We thought in our ignorance prior to this that there could not be anything in the world like the stage child, but you see we were mistaken.

The stage child is affectionate to its parents and its nurse and is respectful in its demeanor toward those whom Providence has placed in authority over it; and so far it is certainly much to be preferred to the real article. It speaks of its male and female progenitors as "dear, dear papa" and "dear, dear mamma," and it refers to its nurse as "darling nursey." We are connected with a youthful child ourselves--a real one--a nephew. He alludes to his father (when his father is not present) as "the old man," and always calls the nurse "old nut-crackers." Why cannot they make real children who say "dear, dear mamma" and "dear, dear papa?"

The stage child is much superior to the live infant in every way. The stage child does not go rampaging about a house and screeching and yelling till nobody knows whether they are on their heads or their heels.

A stage child does not get up at five o'clock in the morning to practice playing on a penny whistle. A stage child never wants a bicycle and drives you mad about it. A stage child does not ask twenty complicated questions a minute about things that you don't understand, and then wind up by asking why you don't seem to know anything, and why wouldn't anybody teach you anything when you were a little boy.

The stage child does not wear a hole in the seat of its knickerbockers and have to have a patch let in. The stage child comes downstairs on its feet.

The stage child never brings home six other children to play at horses in the front garden, and then wants to know if they can all come in to tea. The stage child never has the wooping-cough, and the measles, and every other disease that it can lay its hands on, and be laid up with them one after the other and turn the house upside down.

The stage child's department in the scheme of life is to harrow up its mother's feelings by ill-timed and uncalled-for questions about its father. It always wants to know, before a roomful of people, where "dear papa" is, and why he has left dear mamma; when, as all the guests know, the poor man is doing his two years' hard or waiting to be hanged. It makes everybody so uncomfortable.

It is always harrowing up somebody--the stage child; it really ought not to be left about as it is. When it has done upsetting its mother it fishes out some broken-hearted maid, who has just been cruelly severed forever from her lover, and asks her in a high falsetto voice why she doesn't get married, and prattles to her about love, and domestic bliss, and young men, and any other subject it can think of particularly calculated to lacerate the poor girl's heart until her brain nearly gives way.

After that it runs amuck up and down the whole play and makes everybody sit up all round. It asks eminently respectable old maids if they wouldn't like to have a baby; and it wants to know why bald-headed old men have left off wearing hair, and why other old gentlemen have red noses and if they were always that color.

In some plays it so happens that the less said about the origin and source of the stage child the better; and in such cases nothing will appear so important to that contrary brat as to know, in the middle of an evening-party, who its father was!

Everybody loves the stage child. They catch it up in their bosoms every other minute and weep over it. They take it in turns to do this.

Nobody--on the stage, we mean--ever has enough of the stage child. Nobody ever tells the stage child to "shut up" or to "get out of this." Nobody ever clumps the stage child over the head.

When the real child goes to the theater it must notice these things and wish it were a stage child.

The stage child is much admired by the audience. Its pathos makes them weep; its tragedy thrills them; its declamation--as for instance when it takes the center of the stage and says it will kill the wicked man, and the police, and everybody who hurts its mar--stirs them like a trumpet note; and its light comedy is generally held to be the most truly humorous thing in the whole range of dramatic art.

But there are some people so strangely constituted that they do not appreciate the stage child; they do not comprehend its uses; they do not understand its beauties. We should not be angry with them. We should the rather pity them.

We ourselves had a friend once who suffered from this misfortune. He was a married man, and Providence had been very gracious, very good to him: he had been blessed with eleven children, and they were all growing up well and strong.

The "baby" was eleven weeks old, and then came the twins, who were getting on for fifteen months and were cutting their double teeth nicely. The youngest girl was three; there were five boys aged seven, eight, nine, ten, and twelve respectively--good enough lads, but--well, there, boys will be boys, you know; we were just the same ourselves when we were young. The two eldest were both very pleasant girls, as their mother said; the only pity was that they would quarrel so with each other.

We never knew a healthier set of boys and girls. They were so full of energy and dash.

Our friend was very much out of sorts one evening when we called on him. It was holiday-time and wet weather. He had been at home all day, and so had all the children. He was telling his wife when we entered the room that if the holidays were to last much longer and those twins did not hurry up and get their teeth quickly, he should have to go away and join the County Council. He could not stand the racket.

His wife said she could not see what he had to complain of. She was sure better-hearted children no man could have.

Our friend said he didn't care a straw about their hearts. It was their legs and arms and lungs that were driving him crazy.

He also said that he would go out with us and get away from it for a bit, or he should go mad.

He proposed a theater, and we accordingly made our way toward the Strand. Our friend, in closing the door behind him, said he could not tell us what a relief it was to get away from those children. He said he loved children very much indeed, but that it was a mistake to have too much of anything, however much you liked it, and that he had come to the conclusion that twenty-two hours a day of them was enough for any one.

He said he did not want to see another child or hear another child until he got home. He wanted to forget that there were such things as children in the world.

We got up to the Strand and dropped into the first theater we came to. The curtain went up, and on the stage was a small child standing in its nightshirt and screaming for its mother.

Our friend looked, said one word and bolted, and we followed.

We went a little further and dropped into another theater.

Here there were two children on the stage. Some grown-up people were standing round them listening, in respectful attitudes, while the children talked. They appeared to be lecturing about something.

Again we fled, swearing, and made our way to a third theater. They were all children there. It was somebody or other's Children's Company performing an opera, or pantomime, or something of that sort.

Our friend said he would not venture into another theater. He said he had heard there were places called music-halls, and he begged us to take him to one of these and not to tell his wife.

We inquired of a policeman and found that there really were such places, and we took him into one.

The first thing we saw were two little boys doing tricks on a horizontal bar.

Our friend was about to repeat his customary programme of flying and cursing, but we restrained him. We assured him that he would really see a grown-up person if he waited a bit, so he sat out the boys and also their little sister on a bicycle and waited for the next item.

It turned out to be an infant phenomenon who sang and danced in fourteen different costumes, and we once more fled.

Our friend said he could not go home in the state he was then; he felt sure he should kill the twins if he did. He pondered for awhile, and then he thought he would go and hear some music. He said he thought a little music would soothe and ennoble him--make him feel more like a Christian than he did at that precise moment.

We were near St. James' Hall, so we went in there.

The hall was densely crowded, and we had great difficulty in forcing our way to our seats. We reached them at length, and then turned our eyes toward the orchestra.

"The marvelous boy pianist--only ten years old!" was giving a recital.

Then our friend rose and said he thought he would give it up and go home.

We asked him if he would like to try any other place of amusement, but he said "No." He said that when you came to think of it, it seemed a waste of money for a man with eleven children of his own to go about to places of entertainment nowadays.

THE COMIC LOVERS.

Oh, they are funny! The comic lovers' mission in life is to serve as a sort of "relief" to the misery caused the audience by the other characters in the play; and all that is wanted now is something that will be a relief to the comic lovers.

They have nothing to do with the play, but they come on immediately after anything very sad has happened and make love. This is why we watch sad scenes on the stage with such patience. We are not eager for them to be got over. Maybe they are very uninteresting scenes, as well as sad ones, and they make us yawn; but we have no desire to see them hurried through. The longer they take the better pleased we are: we know that when they are finished the comic lovers will come on.

They are always very rude to each other, the comic lovers. Everybody is more or less rude and insulting to every body else on the stage; they call it repartee there! We tried the effect of a little stage "repartee" once upon some people in real life, and we wished we hadn't afterward. It was too subtle for them. They summoned us before a magistrate for "using language calculated to cause a breach of the peace." We were fined 2 pounds and costs!

They are more lenient to "wit and humor" on the stage, and know how to encourage the art of vituperation. But the comic lovers carry the practice almost to excess. They are more than rude--they are abusive. They insult each other from morning to night. What their married life will be like we shudder to think!

In the various slanging matches and bullyragging competitions which form their courtship it is always the maiden that is most successful. Against her merry flow of invective and her girlish wealth of offensive personalities the insolence and abuse of her boyish adorer cannot stand for one moment.

To give an idea of how the comic lovers woo, we perhaps cannot do better than subjoin the following brief example:

    SCENE: Main thoroughfare in populous district of London. Time: Noon. Not a soul to be seen anywhere.

    Enter comic loveress R., walking in the middle of the road.

    Enter comic lover L., also walking in the middle of the road.

    They neither see the other until they bump against each other in the center.

HE. Why, Jane! Who'd a' thought o' meeting you here!

SHE. You evidently didn't--stoopid!

HE. Halloo! got out o' bed the wrong side again? I say, Jane, if you go on like that you'll never get a man to marry you.

SHE. So I thought when I engaged myself to you.

HE. Oh! come, Jane, don't be hard.

SHE. Well, one of us must be hard. You're soft enough.

HE. Yes, I shouldn't want to marry you if I weren't. Ha! ha! ha!

SHE. Oh, you gibbering idiot! (Said archly.)

HE. So glad I am. We shall make a capital match (attempts to kiss her).

SHE (slipping away). Yes, and you'll find I'm a match that can strike (fetches him a violent blow over the side if the head).

HE (holding his jaw--in a literal sense, we mean). I can't help feeling smitten by her.

SHE. Yes, I'm a bit of a spanker, ain't I?

HE. Spanker. I call you a regular stunner. You've nearly made me silly.

SHE (laughing playfully). No, nature did that for you, Joe, long ago.

HE. Ah, well, you've made me smart enough now, you boss-eyed old cow, you!

SHE. Cow! am I? Ah, I suppose that's what makes me so fond of a calf, you German sausage on legs! You--

HE. Go along. Your mother brought you up on sour milk.

SHE. Yah! They weaned you on thistles, didn't they?

And so on, with such like badinage do they hang about in the middle of that road, showering derision and contumely upon each other for full ten minutes, when, with one culminating burst of mutual abuse, they go off together fighting and the street is left once more deserted.

It is very curious, by the bye, how deserted all public places become whenever a stage character is about. It would seem as though ordinary citizens sought to avoid them. We have known a couple of stage villains to have Waterloo Bridge, Lancaster Place, and a bit of the Strand entirely to themselves for nearly a quarter of an hour on a summer's afternoon while they plotted a most diabolical outrage.

As for Trafalgar Square, the hero always chooses that spot when he wants to get away from the busy crowd and commune in solitude with his own bitter thoughts; and the good old lawyer leaves his office and goes there to discuss any very delicate business over which he particularly does not wish to be disturbed.

And they all make speeches there to an extent sufficient to have turned the hair of the late lamented Sir Charles Warren White with horror. But it is all right, because there is nobody near to hear them. As far as the eye can reach, not a living thing is to be seen. Northumberland Avenue, the Strand, and St. Martin's Lane are simply a wilderness. The only sign of life about is a 'bus at the top of Whitehall, and it appears to be blocked.

How it has managed to get blocked we cannot say. It has the whole road to itself, and is, in fact, itself the only traffic for miles round. Yet there it sticks for hours. The police make no attempt to move it on and the passengers seem quite contented.

The Thames Embankment is an even still more lonesome and desolate part. Wounded (stage) spirits fly from the haunts of men and, leaving the hard, cold world far, far behind them, go and die in peace on the Thames Embankment. And other wanderers, finding their skeletons afterward, bury them there and put up rude crosses over the graves to mark the spot.

The comic lovers are often very young, and when people on the stage are young they *are* young. He is supposed to be about sixteen and she is fifteen. But they both talk as if they were not more than seven.

In real life "boys" of sixteen know a thing or two, we have generally found. The average "boy" of sixteen nowadays usually smokes cavendish and does a little on the Stock Exchange or makes a book; and as for love! he has quite got over it by that age. On the stage, however, the new-born babe is not in it for innocence with the boy lover of sixteen.

So, too, with the maiden. Most girls of fifteen off the stage, so our experience goes, know as much as there is any actual necessity for them to know, Mr. Gilbert notwithstanding; but when we see a young lady of fifteen on the stage we wonder where her cradle is.

The comic lovers do not have the facilities for love-making that the hero and heroine do. The hero and heroine have big rooms to make love in, with a fire and plenty of easy-chairs, so that they can sit about in picturesque attitudes and do it comfortably. Or if they want to do it out of doors they have a ruined abbey, with a big stone seat in the center, and moonlight.

The comic lovers, on the other hand, have to do it standing up all the time, in busy streets, or in cheerless-looking and curiously narrow rooms in which there is no furniture whatever and no fire.

And there is always a tremendous row going on in the house when the comic lovers are making love. Somebody always seems to be putting up pictures in the next room, and putting them up boisterously, too, so that the comic lovers have to shout at each other.

THE PEASANTS.

They are so clean. We have seen peasantry off the stage, and it has presented an untidy--occasionally a disreputable and unwashed--appearance; but the stage peasant seems to spend all his wages on soap and hair-oil.

They are always round the corner--or rather round the two corners--and they come on in a couple of streams and meet in the center; and when they are in their proper position they smile.

There is nothing like the stage peasants' smile in this world--nothing so perfectly inane, so calmly imbecile.

They are so happy. They don't look it, but we know they are because they say so. If you don't believe them, they dance three steps to the right and three steps to the left back again. They can't help it. It is because they are so happy.

When they are more than usually rollicking they stand in a semicircle, with their hands on each other's shoulders, and sway from side to side, trying to make themselves sick. But this is only when they are simply bursting with joy.

Stage peasants never have any work to do.

Sometimes we see them going to work, sometimes coming home from work, but nobody has ever seen them actually at work. They could not afford to work--it would spoil their clothes.

They are very sympathetic, are stage peasants. They never seem to have any affairs of their own to think about, but they make up for this by taking a three-hundred-horse-power interest in things in which they have no earthly concern.

What particularly rouses them is the heroine's love affairs. They could listen to them all day.

They yearn to hear what she said to him and to be told what he replied to her, and they repeat it to each other.

In our own love-sick days we often used to go and relate to various people all the touching conversations that took place between our lady-love and ourselves; but our friends never seemed to get excited over it. On the contrary, a casual observer might even have been led to the idea that they were bored by our recital. And they had trains to catch and men to meet before we had got a quarter through the job.

Ah, how often in those days have we yearned for the sympathy of a stage peasantry, who would have crowded round us, eager not to miss one word of the thrilling narrative, who would have rejoiced with us with an encouraging laugh, and have condoled with us with a grieved "Oh," and who would have gone off, when we had had enough of them, singing about it.

By the way, this is a very beautiful trait in the character of the stage peasantry, their prompt and unquestioning compliance with the slightest wish of any of the principals.

"Leave me, friends," says the heroine, beginning to make preparations for weeping, and before she can turn round they are clean gone--one lot to the right, evidently making for the back entrance of the public-house, and the other half to the left, where they visibly hide themselves behind the pump and wait till somebody else wants them.

The stage peasantry do not talk much, their strong point being to listen. When they cannot get any more information about the state of the heroine's heart, they like to be told long and complicated stories about wrongs done years ago to people that they never heard of. They seem to be able to grasp and understand these stories with ease. This makes the audience envious of them.

When the stage peasantry do talk, however, they soon make up for lost time. They start off all together with a suddenness that nearly knocks you over.

They all talk. Nobody listens. Watch any two of them. They are both talking as hard as they can go. They have been listening quite enough to other people: you can't expect them to listen to each other. But the conversation under such conditions must be very trying.

And then they flirt so sweetly! so idyllicly!

It has been our privilege to see real peasantry flirt, and it has always struck us as a singularly solid and substantial affair--makes one think, somehow, of a steamroller flirting with a cow--but on the stage it is so sylph-like. She has short skirts, and her stockings are so much tidier and better fitting than these things are in real peasant life, and she is arch and coy. She turns away from him and laughs--such a silvery laugh. And he is ruddy and curly haired and has on such a beautiful waistcoat! how can she help but love him? And he is so tender and devoted and holds her by the waist; and she slips round and comes up the other side. Oh, it is so bewitching!

The stage peasantry like to do their love-making as much in public as possible. Some people fancy a place all to themselves for this sort of thing--where nobody else is about. We ourselves do. But the stage peasant is more sociably inclined. Give him the village green, just outside the public-house, or the square on market-day to do his spooning in.

They are very faithful, are stage peasants. No jilting, no fickleness, no breach of promise. If the gentleman in pink walks out with the lady in blue in the first act, pink and blue will be married in the end. He sticks to her all through and she sticks to him.

Girls in yellow may come and go, girls in green may laugh and dance--the gentleman in pink heeds them not. Blue is his color, and he never leaves it. He stands beside it, he sits beside it. He drinks with her, he smiles with her, he laughs with her, he dances with her, he comes on with her, he goes off with her.

When the time comes for talking he talks to her and only her, and she talks to him and only him. Thus there is no jealousy, no quarreling. But we should prefer an occasional change ourselves.

There are no married people in stage villages and no children (consequently, of course-happy village! oh, to discover it and spend a month there!). There are just the same number of men as there are women in all stage villages, and they are all about the same age and each young man loves some young woman. But they never marry.

They talk a lot about it, but they never do it. The artful beggars! They see too much what it's like among the principals.

The stage peasant is fond of drinking, and when he drinks he likes to let you know he is drinking. None of your quiet half-pint inside the bar for him. He likes to come out in the street and sing about it and do tricks with it, such as turning it topsy-turvy over his head.

Notwithstanding all this he is moderate, mind you. You can't say he takes too much. One small jug of ale among forty is his usual allowance.

He has a keen sense of humor and is easily amused. There is something almost pathetic about the way he goes into convulsions of laughter over such very small jokes. How a man like that would enjoy a real joke! One day he will perhaps hear a real joke. Who knows? It will, however, probably kill him. One grows to love the stage peasant after awhile. He is so good, so child-like, so unworldly. He realizes one's ideal of Christianity.

THE GOOD OLD MAN.

He has lost his wife. But he knows where she is--among the angels! She isn't all gone, because the heroine has her hair. "Ah, you've got your mother's hair," says the good old man, feeling the girl's head all over as she kneels beside him. Then they all wipe away a tear.

The people on the stage think very highly of the good old man, but they don't encourage him much after the first act. He generally dies in the first act.

If he does not seem likely to die they murder him.

He is a most unfortunate old gentleman. Anything he is mixed up in seems bound to go wrong. If he is manager or director of a bank, smash it goes before even one act is over. His particular firm is always on the verge of bankruptcy. We have only to be told that he has put all his savings into a company--no matter how sound and promising an affair it may always have been and may still seem--to know that that company is a "goner."

No power on earth can save it after once the good old man has become a shareholder.

If we lived in stage-land and were asked to join any financial scheme, our first question would be:

"Is the good old man in it?" If so, that would decide us.

When the good old man is a trustee for any one he can battle against adversity much longer. He is a plucky old fellow, and while that trust money lasts he keeps a brave heart and fights on boldly. It is not until he has spent the last penny of it that he gives way.

It then flashes across the old man's mind that his motives for having lived in luxury upon that trust money for years may possibly be misunderstood. The world--the hollow, heartless world--will call it a swindle and regard him generally as a

Stage-Land

precious old fraud.

This idea quite troubles the good old man.

But the world really ought not to blame him. No one, we are sure, could be more ready and willing to make amends (when found out); and to put matters right he will cheerfully sacrifice his daughter's happiness and marry her to the villain.

The villain, by the way, has never a penny to bless himself with, and cannot even pay his own debts, let alone helping anybody else out of a scrape. But the good old man does not think of this.

Our own personal theory, based upon a careful comparison of similarities, is that the good old man is in reality the stage hero grown old. There is something about the good old man's chuckle-headed simplicity, about his helpless imbecility, and his irritating damtom foolishness that is strangely suggestive of the hero.

He is just the sort of old man that we should imagine the hero would develop into.

We may, of course, be wrong; but that is our idea.

THE IRISHMAN.

He says "Shure" and "Bedad" and in moments of exultation "Beghorra." That is all the Irish he knows.

He is very poor, but scrupulously honest. His great ambition is to pay his rent, and he is devoted to his landlord.

He is always cheerful and always good. We never knew a bad Irishman on the stage. Sometimes a stage Irishman seems to be a bad man--such as the "agent" or the "informer"--but in these cases it invariably turns out in the end that this man was all along a Scotchman, and thus what had been a mystery becomes clear and explicable.

The stage Irishman is always doing the most wonderful things imaginable. We do not see him do those wonderful things. He does them when nobody is by and tells us all about them afterward: that is how we know of them.

We remember on one occasion, when we were young and somewhat inexperienced, planking our money down and going into a theater solely and purposely to see the stage Irishman do the things he was depicted as doing on the posters outside.

They were really marvelous, the things he did on that poster.

In the right-hand upper corner he appeared running across country on all fours, with a red herring sticking out from his coat-tails, while far behind came hounds and horsemen hunting him. But their chance of ever catching him up was clearly hopeless.

To the left he was represented as running away over one of the wildest and most rugged bits of landscape we have ever seen with a very big man on his back. Six policemen stood scattered about a mile behind him. They had evidently been running after him, but had at last given up the pursuit as useless.

In the center of the poster he was having a friendly fight with seventeen ladies and gentlemen. Judging from the costumes, the affair appeared to be a wedding. A few of the guests had already been killed and lay dead about the floor. The survivors, however, were enjoying themselves immensely, and of all that gay group he was the gayest.

At the moment chosen by the artist, he had just succeeded in cracking the bridegroom's skull.

"We must see this," said we to ourselves. "This is good." And we had a bob's worth.

But he did not do any of the things that we have mentioned, after all--at least, we mean we did not see him do any of them. It seems he did them "off," and then came on and told his mother all about it afterward.

He told it very well, but somehow or other we were disappointed. We had so reckoned on that fight.

By the bye, we have noticed, even among the characters of real life, a tendency to perform most of their wonderful feats "off."

It has been our privilege since then to gaze upon many posters on which have been delineated strange and moving stage events.

We have seen the hero holding the villain up high above his head, and throwing him about that carelessly that we have felt afraid he would break something with him.

We have seen a heroine leaping from the roof of a house on one side of the street and being caught by the comic man standing on the roof of a house on the other side of the street and thinking nothing of it.

We have seen railway trains rushing into each other at the rate of sixty miles an hour. We have seen houses blown up by dynamite two hundred feet into the air. We have seen the defeat of the Spanish Armada, the destruction of Pompeii, and the return of the British army from Egypt in one "set" each.

Such incidents as earthquakes, wrecks in mid-ocean, revolutions and battles we take no note of, they being commonplace and ordinary.

But we do not go inside to see these things now. We have two looks at the poster instead; it is more satisfying.

The Irishman, to return to our friend, is very fond of whisky--the stage Irishman, we mean. Whisky is forever in his thoughts--and often in other places belonging to him, besides.

The fashion in dress among stage Irishmen is rather picturesque than neat. Tailors must have a hard time of it in stage Ireland.

The stage Irishman has also an original taste in hats. He always wears a hat without a crown; whether to keep his head cool or with any political significance we cannot say.

THE DETECTIVE.

Ah! he is a cute one, he is. Possibly in real life he would not be deemed anything extraordinary, but by contrast with the average of stage men and women, any one who is not a born fool naturally appears somewhat Machiavellian.

He is the only man in the play who does not swallow all the villain tells him and believe it, and come up with his mouth open for more. He is the only man who can see through the disguise of an overcoat and a new hat.

There is something very wonderful about the disguising power of cloaks and hats upon the stage. This comes from the habit people on the stage have of recognizing their friends, not by their faces and voices, but by their cloaks and hats.

A married man on the stage knows his wife, because he knows she wears a blue ulster and a red bonnet. The moment she leaves off that blue ulster and red bonnet he is lost and does not know where she is.

She puts on a yellow cloak and a green hat, and coming in at another door says she is a lady from the country, and does he want a housekeeper?

Having lost his beloved wife, and feeling that there is no one now to keep the children quiet, he engages her. She puzzles him a good deal, this new housekeeper. There is something about her that strangely reminds him of his darling Nell--maybe her boots and dress, which she has not had time to change.

Sadly the slow acts pass away until one day, as it is getting near closing-time, she puts on the blue ulster and the red bonnet again and comes in at the old original door.

Then he recognizes her and asks her where she has been all these cruel years.

Even the bad people, who as a rule do possess a little sense--indeed, they are the only persons in the play who ever pretend to any--are deceived by singularly thin disguises.

The detective comes in to their secret councils, with his hat drawn down over his eyes, and followed by the hero speaking in a squeaky voice; and the villains mistake them for members of the band and tell them all their plans.

If the villains can't get themselves found out that way, then they go into a public tea-garden and recount their crimes to one another in a loud tone of voice.

They evidently think that it is only fair to give the detective a chance.

The detective must not be confounded with the policeman. The stage policeman is always on the side of the villain; the detective backs virtue.

The stage detective is, in fact, the earthly agent of a discerning and benevolent Providence. He stands by and allows vice to be triumphant and the good people to be persecuted for awhile without interference. Then when he considers that we have all had about enough of it (to which conclusion, by the bye, he arrives somewhat late) he comes forward, handcuffs the bad people, sorts out and gives back to the good people all their various estates and wives, promises the chief villain twenty years' penal servitude, and all is joy.

THE SAILOR.

He does suffer so with his trousers. He has to stop and pull them up about twice every minute.

One of these days, if he is not careful, there will be an accident happen to those trousers.

If the stage sailor will follow our advice, he will be warned in time and will get a pair of braces.

Sailors in real life do not have nearly so much trouble with their trousers as sailors on the stage do. Why is this? We have seen a good deal of sailors in real life, but on only one occasion, that we can remember, did we ever see a real sailor pull his trousers up.

And then he did not do it a bit like they do it on the stage.

The stage sailor places his right hand behind him and his left in front, leaps up into the air, kicks out his leg behind in a gay and bird-like way, and the thing is done.

The real sailor that we saw began by saying a bad word. Then he leaned up against a brick wall and undid his belt, pulled up his "bags" as he stood there (he never attempted to leap up into the air), tucked in his jersey, shook his legs, and walked on.

It was a most unpicturesque performance to watch.

The thing that the stage sailor most craves in this life is that somebody should shiver his timbers.

"Shiver my timbers!" is the request he makes to every one he meets. But nobody ever does it.

His chief desire with regard to the other people in the play is that they should "belay there, avast!" We do not know how this is done; but the stage sailor is a good and kindly man, and we feel convinced he would not recommend the exercise if it were not conducive to piety and health.

The stage sailor is good to his mother and dances the hornpipe beautifully. We have never found a real sailor who could dance a hornpipe, though we have made extensive inquiries throughout the profession. We were introduced to a ship's steward who offered to do us a cellar-flap for a pot of four-half, but that was not what we wanted.

The stage sailor is gay and rollicking: the real sailors we have met have been, some of them, the most worthy and single-minded of men, but they have appeared sedate rather than gay, and they haven't rollicked much.

The stage sailor seems to have an easy time of it when at sea. The hardest work we have ever seen him do then has been folding up a rope or dusting the sides of the ship.

But it is only in his very busy moments that he has to work to this extent; most of his time is occupied in chatting with the captain.

By the way, speaking of the sea, few things are more remarkable in their behavior than a stage sea. It must be difficult to navigate in a stage sea, the currents are so confusing.

As for the waves, there is no knowing how to steer for them; they are so tricky. At one moment they are all on the larboard, the sea on the other side of the vessel being perfectly calm, and the next instant they have crossed over and are all on the starboard, and before the captain can think how to meet this new dodge, the whole ocean has slid round and got itself into a heap at the back of him.

Seamanship is useless against such very unprofessional conduct as this, and the vessel is wrecked.

A wreck at (stage) sea is a truly awful sight. The thunder and lightning never leave off for an instant; the crew run round and round the mast and scream; the heroine, carrying the stage child in her arms and with her back hair down, rushes about and gets in everybody's way. The comic man alone is calm!

The next instant the bulwarks fall down flat on the deck and the mast goes straight up into the sky and disappears, then the water reaches the powder magazine and there is a terrific explosion.

This is followed by a sound as of linen sheets being ripped up, and the passengers and crew hurry downstairs into the cabin, evidently with the idea of getting out of the way of the sea, which has climbed up and is now level with the deck.

The next moment the vessel separates in the middle and goes off R. and L., so as to make room for a small boat containing the heroine, the child, the comic man, and one sailor.

The way small boats are managed at (stage) sea is even more wonderful than the way in which ships are sailed.

To begin with, everybody sits sideways along the middle of the boat, all facing the starboard. They do not attempt to row. One man does all the work with one scull. This scull he puts down through the water till it touches the bed of the ocean, and then he shoves.

"Deep-sea punting" would be the technical term for the method, we presume.

In this way do they toil--or rather, to speak correctly, does the one man toil--through the awful night, until with joy they see before them the light-house rocks.

The light-house keeper comes out with a lantern. The boat is run in among the breakers and all are saved.

And then the band plays.

www.bookjungle.com *email: sales@bookjungle.com fax: 630-214-0564 mail: Book Jungle PO Box 2226 Champaign, IL 61825*

The Codes Of Hammurabi And Moses
W. W. Davies

QTY

The discovery of the Hammurabi Code is one of the greatest achievements of archaeology, and is of paramount interest, not only to the student of the Bible, but also to all those interested in ancient history...

Religion   **ISBN:** *1-59462-338-4*   **Pages:**132
MSRP $12.95

The Theory of Moral Sentiments
Adam Smith

QTY

This work from 1749. contains original theories of conscience amd moral judgment and it is the foundation for systemof morals.

Philosophy   **ISBN:** *1-59462-777-0*   **Pages:**536
MSRP $19.95

Jessica's First Prayer
Hesba Stretton

QTY

In a screened and secluded corner of one of the many railway-bridges which span the streets of London there could be seen a few years ago, from five o'clock every morning until half past eight, a tidily set-out coffee-stall, consisting of a trestle and board, upon which stood two large tin cans, with a small fire of charcoal burning under each so as to keep the coffee boiling during the early hours of the morning when the work-people were thronging into the city on their way to their daily toil...

Childrens   **ISBN:** *1-59462-373-2*   **Pages:**84
MSRP $9.95

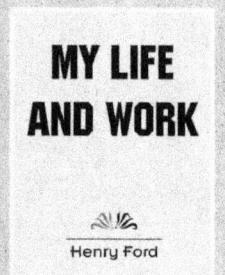

My Life and Work
Henry Ford

QTY

Henry Ford revolutionized the world with his implementation of mass production for the Model T automobile. Gain valuable business insight into his life and work with his own auto-biography... "We have only started on our development of our country we have not as yet, with all our talk of wonderful progress, done more than scratch the surface. The progress has been wonderful enough but..."

Biographies/   **ISBN:** *1-59462-198-5*   **Pages:**300
MSRP $21.95

The Art of Cross-Examination
Francis Wellman

I presume it is the experience of every author, after his first book is published upon an important subject, to be almost overwhelmed with a wealth of ideas and illustrations which could readily have been included in his book, and which to his own mind, at least, seem to make a second edition inevitable. Such certainly was the case with me; and when the first edition had reached its sixth impression in five months, I rejoiced to learn that it seemed to my publishers that the book had met with a sufficiently favorable reception to justify a second and considerably enlarged edition. ..

Reference   ISBN: *1-59462-647-2*   Pages:412   MSRP *$19.95*

On the Duty of Civil Disobedience
Henry David Thoreau

Thoreau wrote his famous essay, On the Duty of Civil Disobedience, as a protest against an unjust but popular war and the immoral but popular institution of slave-owning. He did more than write—he declined to pay his taxes, and was hauled off to gaol in consequence. Who can say how much this refusal of his hastened the end of the war and of slavery ?

Law   ISBN: *1-59462-747-9*   Pages:48   MSRP *$7.45*

Dream Psychology Psychoanalysis for Beginners
Sigmund Freud

Sigmund Freud, born Sigismund Schlomo Freud (May 6, 1856 - September 23, 1939), was a Jewish-Austrian neurologist and psychiatrist who co-founded the psychoanalytic school of psychology. Freud is best known for his theories of the unconscious mind, especially involving the mechanism of repression; his redefinition of sexual desire as mobile and directed towards a wide variety of objects; and his therapeutic techniques, especially his understanding of transference in the therapeutic relationship and the presumed value of dreams as sources of insight into unconscious desires.

Psychology   ISBN: *1-59462-905-6*   Pages:196   MSRP *$15.45*

The Miracle of Right Thought
Orison Swett Marden

Believe with all of your heart that you will do what you were made to do. When the mind has once formed the habit of holding cheerful, happy, prosperous pictures, it will not be easy to form the opposite habit. It does not matter how improbable or how far away this realization may see, or how dark the prospects may be, if we visualize them as best we can, as vividly as possible, hold tenaciously to them and vigorously struggle to attain them, they will gradually become actualized, realized in the life. But a desire, a longing without endeavor, a yearning abandoned or held indifferently will vanish without realization.

Self Help   ISBN: *1-59462-644-8*   Pages:360   MSRP *$25.45*

www.bookjungle.com *email: sales@bookjungle.com fax: 630-214-0564 mail: Book Jungle PO Box 2226 Champaign, IL 61825*

QTY

	Title	ISBN	Price
☐	**The Rosicrucian Cosmo-Conception Mystic Christianity** by *Max Heindel*	ISBN: 1-59462-188-8	**$38.95**
	The Rosicrucian Cosmo-conception is not dogmatic, neither does it appeal to any other authority than the reason of the student. It is: not controversial, but is: sent forth in the, hope that it may help to clear...		New Age/Religion Pages 646
☐	**Abandonment To Divine Providence** by *Jean-Pierre de Caussade*	ISBN: 1-59462-228-0	**$25.95**
	"The Rev. Jean Pierre de Caussade was one of the most remarkable spiritual writers of the Society of Jesus in France in the 18th Century. His death took place at Toulouse in 1751. His works have gone through many editions and have been republished...		Inspirational/Religion Pages 400
☐	**Mental Chemistry** by *Charles Haanel*	ISBN: 1-59462-192-6	**$23.95**
	Mental Chemistry allows the change of material conditions by combining and appropriately utilizing the power of the mind. Much like applied chemistry creates something new and unique out of careful combinations of chemicals the mastery of mental chemistry...		New Age Pages 354
☐	**The Letters of Robert Browning and Elizabeth Barret Barrett 1845-1846 vol II** by *Robert Browning* and *Elizabeth Barrett*	ISBN: 1-59462-193-4	**$35.95**
			Biographies Pages 596
☐	**Gleanings In Genesis (volume I)** by *Arthur W. Pink*	ISBN: 1-59462-130-6	**$27.45**
	Appropriately has Genesis been termed "the seed plot of the Bible" for in it we have, in germ form, almost all of the great doctrines which are afterwards fully developed in the books of Scripture which follow...		Religion/Inspirational Pages 420
☐	**The Master Key** by *L. W. de Laurence*	ISBN: 1-59462-001-6	**$30.95**
	In no branch of human knowledge has there been a more lively increase of the spirit of research during the past few years than in the study of Psychology, Concentration and Mental Discipline. The requests for authentic lessons in Thought Control, Mental Discipline and...		New Age/Business Pages 422
☐	**The Lesser Key Of Solomon Goetia** by *L. W. de Laurence*	ISBN: 1-59462-092-X	**$9.95**
	This translation of the first book of the "Lernegton" which is now for the first time made accessible to students of Talismanic Magic was done, after careful collation and edition, from numerous Ancient Manuscripts in Hebrew, Latin, and French...		New Age/Occult Pages 92
☐	**Rubaiyat Of Omar Khayyam** by *Edward Fitzgerald*	ISBN: 1-59462-332-5	**$13.95**
	Edward Fitzgerald, whom the world has already learned, in spite of his own efforts to remain within the shadow of anonymity, to look upon as one of the rarest poets of the century, was born at Bredfield, in Suffolk, on the 31st of March, 1809. He was the third son of John Purcell...		Music Pages 172
☐	**Ancient Law** by *Henry Maine*	ISBN: 1-59462-128-4	**$29.95**
	The chief object of the following pages is to indicate some of the earliest ideas of mankind, as they are reflected in Ancient Law, and to point out the relation of those ideas to modern thought.		Religiom/History Pages 452
☐	**Far-Away Stories** by *William J. Locke*	ISBN: 1-59462-129-2	**$19.45**
	"Good wine needs no bush, but a collection of mixed vintages does. And this book is just such a collection. Some of the stories I do not want to remain buried for ever in the museum files of dead magazine-numbers an author's not unpardonable vanity..."		Fiction Pages 272
☐	**Life of David Crockett** by *David Crockett*	ISBN: 1-59462-250-7	**$27.45**
	"Colonel David Crockett was one of the most remarkable men of the times in which he lived. Born in humble life, but gifted with a strong will, an indomitable courage, and unremitting perseverance...		Biographies/New Age Pages 424
☐	**Lip-Reading** by *Edward Nitchie*	ISBN: 1-59462-206-X	**$25.95**
	Edward B. Nitchie, founder of the New York School for the Hard of Hearing, now the Nitchie School of Lip-Reading, Inc, wrote "LIP-READING Principles and Practice". The development and perfecting of this meritorious work on lip-reading was an undertaking...		How-to Pages 400
☐	**A Handbook of Suggestive Therapeutics, Applied Hypnotism, Psychic Science** by *Henry Munro*	ISBN: 1-59462-214-0	**$24.95**
			Health/New Age/Health/Self-help Pages 376
☐	**A Doll's House: and Two Other Plays** by *Henrik Ibsen*	ISBN: 1-59462-112-8	**$19.95**
	Henrik Ibsen created this classic when in revolutionary 1848 Rome. Introducing some striking concepts in playwriting for the realist genre, this play has been studied the world over.		Fiction/Classics/Plays 308
☐	**The Light of Asia** by *sir Edwin Arnold*	ISBN: 1-59462-204-3	**$13.95**
	In this poetic masterpiece, Edwin Arnold describes the life and teachings of Buddha. The man who was to become known as Buddha to the world was born as Prince Gautama of India but he rejected the worldly riches and abandoned the reigns of power when...		Religion/History/Biographies Pages 170
☐	**The Complete Works of Guy de Maupassant** by *Guy de Maupassant*	ISBN: 1-59462-157-8	**$16.95**
	"For days and days, nights and nights, I had dreamed of that first kiss which was to consecrate our engagement, and I knew not on what spot I should put my lips..."		Fiction/Classics Pages 240
☐	**The Art of Cross-Examination** by *Francis L. Wellman*	ISBN: 1-59462-309-0	**$26.95**
	Written by a renowned trial lawyer, Wellman imparts his experience and uses case studies to explain how to use psychology to extract desired information through questioning.		How-to/Science/Reference Pages 408
☐	**Answered or Unanswered?** by *Louisa Vaughan*	ISBN: 1-59462-248-5	**$10.95**
	Miracles of Faith in China		Religion Pages 112
☐	**The Edinburgh Lectures on Mental Science (1909)** by *Thomas*	ISBN: 1-59462-008-3	**$11.95**
	This book contains the substance of a course of lectures recently given by the writer in the Queen Street Hall, Edinburgh. Its purpose is to indicate the Natural Principles governing the relation between Mental Action and Material Conditions...		New Age/Psychology Pages 148
☐	**Ayesha** by *H. Rider Haggard*	ISBN: 1-59462-301-5	**$24.95**
	Verily and indeed it is the unexpected that happens! Probably if there was one person upon the earth from whom the Editor of this, and of a certain previous history, did not expect to hear again...		Classics Pages 380
☐	**Ayala's Angel** by *Anthony Trollope*	ISBN: 1-59462-352-X	**$29.95**
	The two girls were both pretty, but Lucy who was twenty-one who supposed to be simple and comparatively unattractive, whereas Ayala was credited, as her Bombwhat romantic name might show, with poetic charm and a taste for romance. Ayala when her father died was nineteen...		Fiction Pages 484
☐	**The American Commonwealth** by *James Bryce*	ISBN: 1-59462-286-8	**$34.45**
	An interpretation of American democratic political theory. It examines political mechanics and society from the perspective of Scotsman James Bryce		Politics Pages 572
☐	**Stories of the Pilgrims** by *Margaret P. Pumphrey*	ISBN: 1-59462-116-0	**$17.95**
	This book explores pilgrims religious oppression in England as well as their escape to Holland and eventual crossing to America on the Mayflower, and their early days in New England...		History Pages 268

www.bookjungle.com email: sales@bookjungle.com fax: 630-214-0564 mail: Book Jungle PO Box 2226 Champaign, IL 61825

QTY

The Fasting Cure *by Sinclair Upton* ISBN: *1-59462-222-1* **$13.95**
In the Cosmopolitan Magazine for May, 1910, and in the Contemporary Review (London) for April, 1910, I published an article dealing with my experiences in fasting. I have written a great many magazine articles, but never one which attracted so much attention... New Age/Self Help/Health Pages 164

Hebrew Astrology *by Sepharial* ISBN: *1-59462-308-2* **$13.45**
In these days of advanced thinking it is a matter of common observation that we have left many of the old landmarks behind and that we are now pressing forward to greater heights and to a wider horizon than that which represented the mind-content of our progenitors... Astrology Pages 144

Thought Vibration or The Law of Attraction in the Thought World ISBN: *1-59462-127-6* **$12.95**
by William Walker Atkinson Psychology/Religion Pages 144

Optimism *by Helen Keller* ISBN: *1-59462-108-X* **$15.95**
Helen Keller was blind, deaf, and mute since 19 months old, yet famously learned how to overcome these handicaps, communicate with the world, and spread her lectures promoting optimism. An inspiring read for everyone... Biographies/Inspirational Pages 84

Sara Crewe *by Frances Burnett* ISBN: *1-59462-360-0* **$9.45**
In the first place, Miss Minchin lived in London. Her home was a large, dull, tall one, in a large, dull square, where all the houses were alike, and all the sparrows were alike, and where all the door-knockers made the same heavy sound... Childrens/Classic Pages 88

The Autobiography of Benjamin Franklin *by Benjamin Franklin* ISBN: *1-59462-135-7* **$24.95**
The Autobiography of Benjamin Franklin has probably been more extensively read than any other American historical work, and no other book of its kind has had such ups and downs of fortune. Franklin lived for many years in England, where he was agent... Biographies/History Pages 332

Name	
Email	
Telephone	
Address	
City, State ZIP	

☐ Credit Card   ☐ Check / Money Order

Credit Card Number	
Expiration Date	
Signature	

Please Mail to: Book Jungle
           PO Box 2226
           Champaign, IL 61825
or Fax to: 630-214-0564

ORDERING INFORMATION

web: *www.bookjungle.com*
email: *sales@bookjungle.com*
fax: *630-214-0564*
mail: *Book Jungle PO Box 2226 Champaign, IL 61825*
or PayPal *to sales@bookjungle.com*

Please contact us for bulk discounts

DIRECT-ORDER TERMS

**20% Discount if You Order
Two or More Books**
Free Domestic Shipping!
Accepted: Master Card, Visa,
Discover, American Express

www.ingramcontent.com/pod-product-compliance
Lightning Source LLC
Chambersburg PA
CBHW081328040426
42453CB00013B/2340